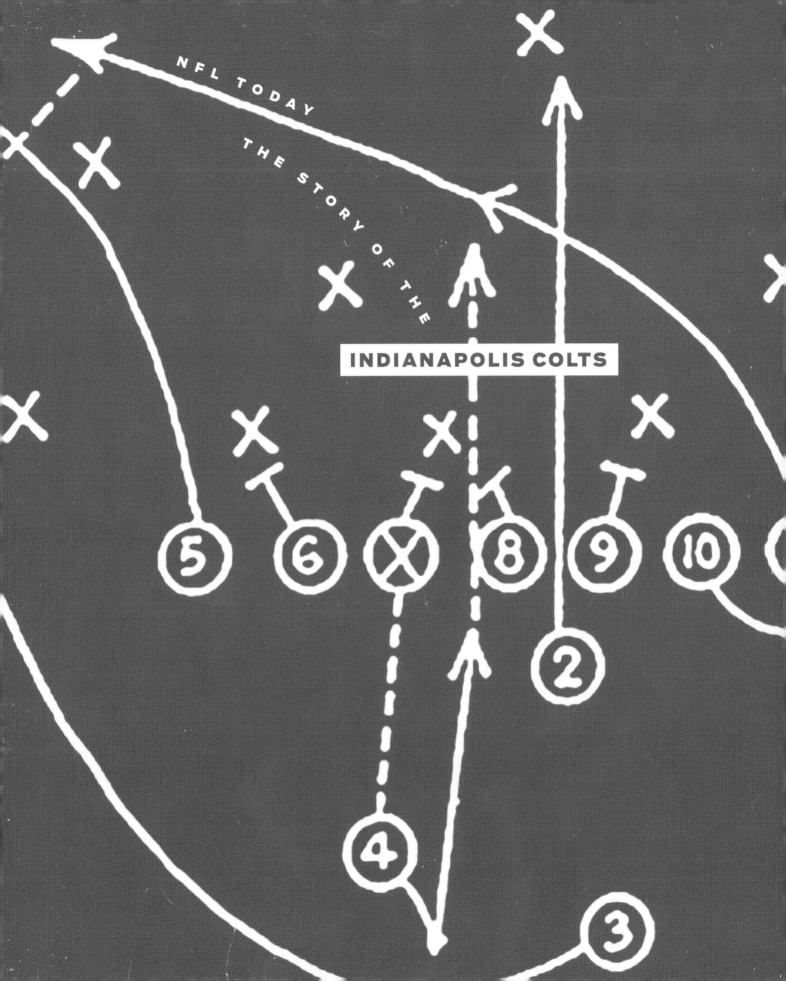

NFL TODAY

THE STORY OF THE INDIANAPOLIS COLTS

SARA GILBERT

CREATIVE EDUCATION

PUBLISHED BY CREATIVE EDUCATION
P.O. BOX 227, MANKATO, MINNESOTA 56002
CREATIVE EDUCATION IS AN IMPRINT OF THE CREATIVE COMPANY
WWW.THECREATIVECOMPANY.US

DESIGN AND PRODUCTION BY BLUE DESIGN
ART DIRECTION BY RITA MARSHALL
PRINTED IN THE UNITED STATES OF AMERICA

PHOTOGRAPHS BY AP IMAGES, CORBIS (BETTMANN, BOHEMIAN NOMAD PICTUREMAKERS, RICHARD CUMMINS), GETTY IMAGES (VERNON BIEVER, KEVIN C. COX, DIAMOND IMAGES, GEORGE GOJKOVICH, CHRIS GRAYTHEN, JEFF GROSS, JEFF HAYNES/AFP, KIDWILER COLLECTION/DIAMOND IMAGES, NICK LAHAM, STREETER LECKA, NEIL LEIFER/SPORTS ILLUSTRATED, ANDY LYONS, BRAD MANGIN/SPORTS ILLUSTRATED, DONALD MIRALLE, NFL, DARRYL NORENBERG/NFL, AL PEREIRA/NFL, SAM RICHE/MCT, JOE ROBBINS, ELIOT SCHECHTER/ALLSPORT, MARC SEROTA, RICK STEWART/ALLSPORT, ROB TRINGALI/SPORTSCHROME, JARED WICKERHAM)

LIBRARY OF CONGRESS CATALOGING-IN-PUBLICATION DATA
GILBERT, SARA.
THE STORY OF THE INDIANAPOLIS COLTS / SARA GILBERT.
P. CM. — (NFL TODAY)
INCLUDES INDEX.
SUMMARY: THE HISTORY OF THE NATIONAL FOOTBALL LEAGUE'S INDIANAPOLIS COLTS, SURVEYING THE FRANCHISE'S BIGGEST STARS AND MOST MEMORABLE MOMENTS FROM ITS INAUGURAL SEASON IN 1953 TO TODAY.
ISBN 978-1-60818-305-0
1. INDIANAPOLIS COLTS (FOOTBALL TEAM)—HISTORY—JUVENILE LITERATURE. I. TITLE.

GV956.I53G55 2013
796.332'640977252—DC23   2012031214

FIRST EDITION
9 8 7 6 5 4 3 2 1

COVER: QUARTERBACK ANDREW LUCK
PAGE 2: DEFENSIVE END ROBERT MATHIS
PAGES 4–5: 2008 INDIANAPOLIS COLTS
PAGE 6: RUNNING BACK JOSEPH ADDAI AND WIDE RECEIVER REGGIE WAYNE

TABLE OF CONTENTS

INDIANAPOLIS HAS BEEN A BIG-TIME FOOTBALL CITY FOR THREE DECADES

Captain of the Colts

When Indiana was granted statehood in 1816, it was told that it needed to establish a capital city. Instead of selecting a town already in existence, the state's legislative leaders decided to build the capital in a swampy area in the middle of the state. In 1821, they named it Indianapolis and marked an area of one square mile for its development. Fewer than 1,000 people lived there, and no one believed that it would ever need more space than that. But today, the sprawling city occupies 372 square miles and is home to more than 800,000 people—making it one of the largest cities in the Midwest.

As the city grew, so did its love of sports. It has hosted the Indianapolis 500, one of the biggest auto-racing events in the country, every year since 1911, and has been home to the Indiana Pacers of the National Basketball Association since 1967. In 1984, football fans in Indiana were given a team to root for as well. The Colts, a National Football League (NFL) franchise from Baltimore, Maryland, moved west to Indianapolis,

GINO MARCHETTI HELPED THE EARLY BALTIMORE COLTS RISE UP AS A LEAGUE POWER

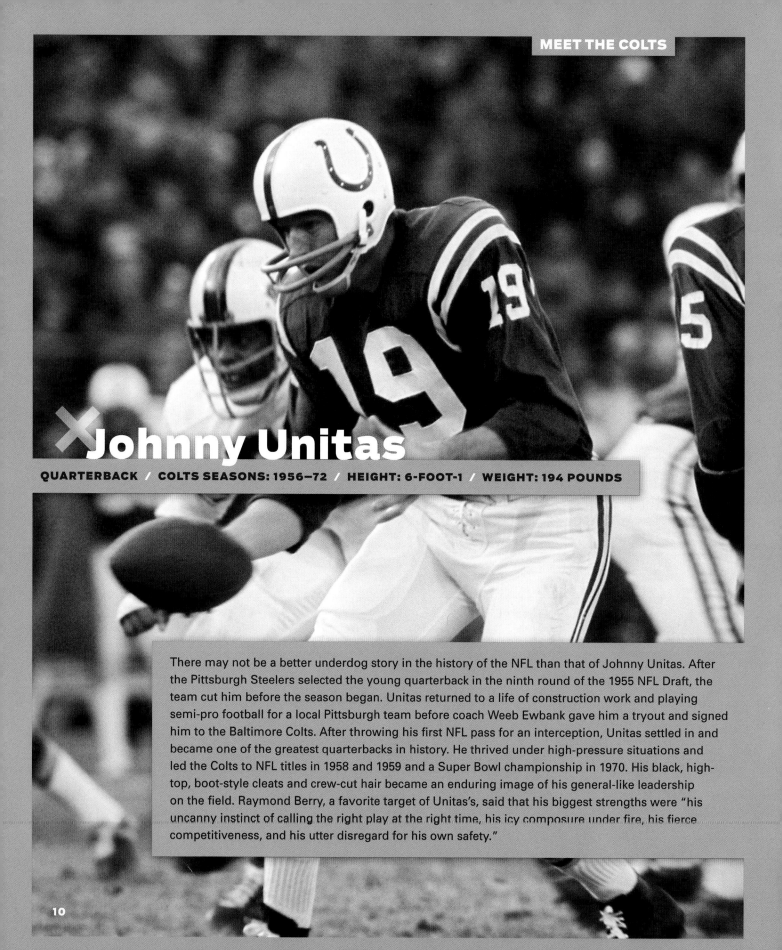

Johnny Unitas

QUARTERBACK / COLTS SEASONS: 1956–72 / HEIGHT: 6-FOOT-1 / WEIGHT: 194 POUNDS

There may not be a better underdog story in the history of the NFL than that of Johnny Unitas. After the Pittsburgh Steelers selected the young quarterback in the ninth round of the 1955 NFL Draft, the team cut him before the season began. Unitas returned to a life of construction work and playing semi-pro football for a local Pittsburgh team before coach Weeb Ewbank gave him a tryout and signed him to the Baltimore Colts. After throwing his first NFL pass for an interception, Unitas settled in and became one of the greatest quarterbacks in history. He thrived under high-pressure situations and led the Colts to NFL titles in 1958 and 1959 and a Super Bowl championship in 1970. His black, high-top, boot-style cleats and crew-cut hair became an enduring image of his general-like leadership on the field. Raymond Berry, a favorite target of Unitas's, said that his biggest strengths were "his uncanny instinct of calling the right play at the right time, his icy composure under fire, his fierce competitiveness, and his utter disregard for his own safety."

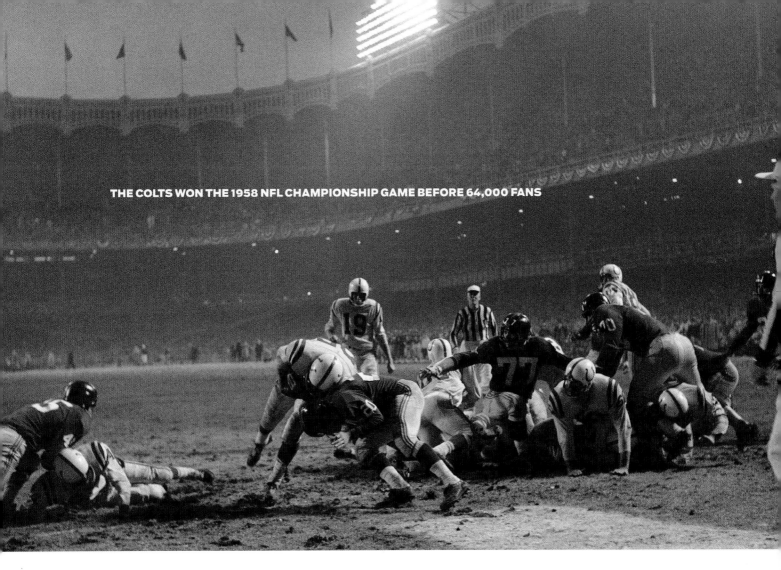

THE COLTS WON THE 1958 NFL CHAMPIONSHIP GAME BEFORE 64,000 FANS

bringing a long and proud tradition with them. As they settled in a new city, they quickly won over new fans in Indiana.

The Colts had become fast fan favorites in Baltimore as well. They played their first season in 1953 and were led early on by veteran NFL coach Weeb Ewbank. During their first three seasons, the Colts went a combined 11–24–1. The team had a few talented players, including running back Claude "Buddy" Young and defensive back Bert Rechichar, and a defensive line that was anchored by tackle Art Donovan and defensive end Gino Marchetti. But the Colts lacked an on-field leader.

That leader showed up in training camp before the 1956 season, hoping for a tryout. Johnny Unitas impressed the coaching staff so much that they quickly added the tough young passer to the roster. Early in the 1956 season, Baltimore's starting quarterback broke his leg. Unitas stepped in and quickly established himself as a star with a knack for producing comeback victories.

Unitas led the Colts to a 7–5 record in 1957. In 1958, Baltimore jumped to a 9–3 record. By then, the team's high-powered offense featured Unitas, bruising fullback Alan Ameche, and sure-handed receivers

Lenny Moore and Raymond Berry. These players led the charge as the young Colts battled all the way to the 1958 NFL Championship Game, where they faced the New York Giants. Baltimore won the thrilling, back-and-forth contest 23–17 on an overtime touchdown plunge by Ameche, making the Colts NFL champions after only six seasons of play.

In 1959, the Colts again met the Giants in the championship game. It was a close contest until Unitas sparked the Colts to 24 fourth-quarter points and a 31–16 win. That performance solidified the legend of "Johnny U." "You can't intimidate him," said Los Angeles Rams defensive tackle Merlin Olsen. "He waits until the last possible second to release the ball, even if it means he's going to take a good lick. When he sees us coming, he knows it's going to hurt, and we know it's going to hurt. But he just stands there and takes it. No other quarterback has such class."

The Colts struggled during the early 1960s, posting mediocre records. After the 1962 season, Coach Ewbank was fired, and Don Shula, who had played for the Colts as a defensive back during the team's inaugural 1953 season, became the new head coach. Coach Shula's first task was to improve the defense. Although the team had several talented defenders, including linebacker Don Shinnick, it needed a spark. With an influx of young talent that included tight end John Mackey and rookie fullback Tony Lorick, Shula guided Unitas and the Colts to an 11-game winning streak in 1964. Baltimore won the Western Conference championship with a 12–2 record but lost in the NFL Championship Game to the Cleveland Browns, 27–0.

In 1965, Baltimore drafted hard-hitting linebacker Mike "Mad Dog" Curtis out of Duke University. Curtis made an immediate impact on the Colts—and on opposing players. "We were playing Green Bay," Baltimore linebacker Ted Hendricks later recalled. "[Packers running back] Jim Grabowski was coming through the line, and Mike Curtis gave him a good old-fashioned clothesline shot. Grabowski got up wobbly. One of our guys handed him his helmet. He started heading for our bench. I tapped him on the shoulder and turned him around and said, 'Yours is on the other side, Jim.'" With Curtis knocking

Birth of the Colts

In 1946, a group of investors purchased the Miami Seahawks, a failing team from the All-America Football Conference (AAFC), and brought them to Baltimore. In an effort to help Baltimore embrace its new team, the new ownership asked fans to rename the franchise. Charles Evans, a Maryland native, won a naming contest with his suggestion to dub the team the "Baltimore Colts," with a horseshoe as its logo. The name was selected as a tribute to Baltimore's proud tradition and history of horse racing. The Preakness Stakes, one of the most prestigious horse races, is held in Baltimore each May. Unfortunately, after the AAFC merged with the NFL in 1950, the Colts posted a miserable 1–11 record, and the league dissolved the team because of its lack of financial stability. Two years went by without professional football in Baltimore. Then, in December 1952, NFL commissioner Bert Bell challenged Baltimore to sell 15,000 season tickets in just 6 weeks. Loyal fans reached that quota in 4 weeks and 3 days, and the Colts were back in business in Baltimore!

THE 1953 COLTS WERE SLUGGISH OUT OF THE GATE, WINNING ONLY THREE GAMES

MIKE CURTIS WAS A TEAM CAPTAIN FOR MOST OF HIS 11 COLTS SEASONS

opponents silly on defense and the veteran Unitas guiding the offense, Baltimore made it to the playoffs again. This time the Colts lost to the Packers, 13–10.

The Colts went 13–1 and won the NFL championship in 1968, and then they won the Super Bowl after the 1970 season. They made the playoffs in 1971 but were beaten by the Miami Dolphins. That was the last hurrah for many of the great Colts players of the '60s. When the Colts finished the 1972 season 5–9, it was clear that the team needed some new blood. After the season, new team owner Robert Irsay decided to trade Unitas to the San Diego Chargers. At the time Unitas left Baltimore, he was the NFL's all-time leader in pass completions (2,796), passing yards (39,768), and touchdown passes (287).

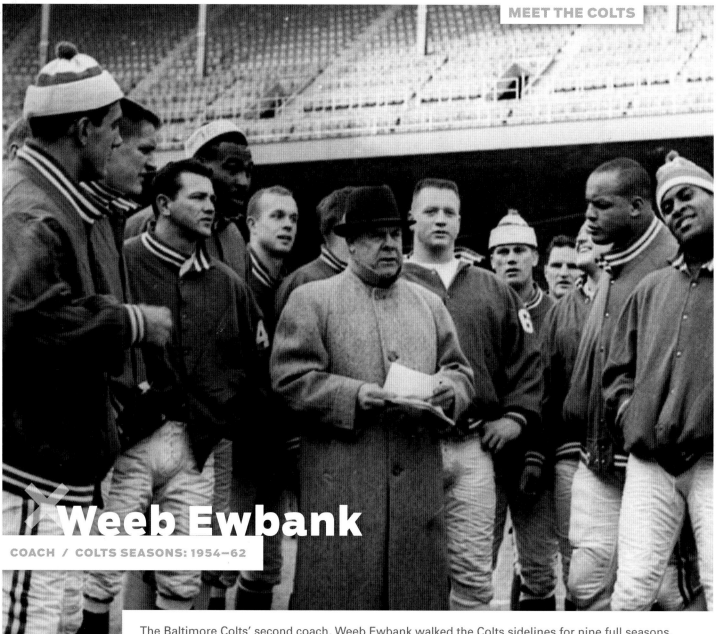

Weeb Ewbank

The Baltimore Colts' second coach, Weeb Ewbank walked the Colts sidelines for nine full seasons. Ewbank was well known for his ability to groom raw, young talent into skilled football players—a knack that made him especially instrumental in the career of quarterback great Johnny Unitas. Ewbank was a master game planner and portrayed a calm demeanor during the week. That wasn't the case on game days, though. During games, Ewbank would be so jittery that he'd chew ice and spit out the pieces as he watched his game plan unfold in front of him. Ewbank led the Colts to two NFL championships, including the 1958 title game that is commonly called "The Greatest Game Ever Played." After leaving the Colts in 1963, Ewbank went on to coach the New York Jets to a shocking victory over the Colts in Super Bowl III, becoming the only coach to win both NFL and American Football League (AFL) championship titles as well as a Super Bowl. "I played under 9 head coaches and 42 assistants," recalled Jets Hall of Fame wide receiver Don Maynard, "and nobody ever did it as good as Weeb."

The Greatest Game Ever Played

Most football games last only until the clock runs out. But the 1958 NFL Championship Game between the Baltimore Colts and the New York Giants would remain in the memories of football fans for decades. Still known to this day as "The Greatest Game Ever Played," this famous showdown took place on December 28 at Yankee Stadium in New York City. With only two minutes left in the game and the Giants leading 17–14, the Colts had the ball on their own 14-yard line. Colts quarterback Johnny Unitas, who excelled in high-pressure situations, engineered a drive that allowed kicker Steve Myhra to boot the tying field goal with just seven seconds left. America was about to witness the very first NFL Championship Game to be decided by sudden-death overtime. After holding the Giants in overtime, the Colts drove 80 yards to score on a 1-yard run by running back Alan Ameche. Watched by millions of fans on television, The Greatest Game Ever Played was credited with sparking broad interest in professional football and helping it become arguably the most popular spectator sport in America.

COLTS KICKER STEVE MYHRA CONTRIBUTED A FIELD GOAL IN THE 1958 TITLE GAME

Riding West

In 1973, the Colts found their new quarterback in the NFL Draft, selecting Louisiana State University star Bert Jones. The young quarterback spent his first two seasons on the bench, but by 1975, he was ready to step into the starting role. Jones proved to be a worthy replacement for the great Unitas when he led the Colts to a 10–4 record and their first American Football Conference (AFC) East Division title.

Jones quickly earned the respect of his teammates by displaying both his leadership and toughness. In one 1976 game, Jones led the Colts to a victory over the Houston Oilers despite having a terrible case of the flu. "He was so sick yesterday that I thought he'd fall down if an Oiler so much as breathed on him," said Baltimore offensive lineman George Kunz after the game. "But he played another great game. He's tough. It kind of rubs off on the rest of us."

BERT JONES WAS CELEBRATED AS THE NFL'S MOST VALUABLE PLAYER IN 1976

Gino Marchetti

DEFENSIVE END / COLTS SEASONS: 1953–64, 1966 / HEIGHT: 6-FOOT-4 / WEIGHT: 244 POUNDS

The last thing a quarterback in the 1950s wanted was a third-and-long situation with Gino Marchetti staring at him from across the line of scrimmage. For more than a decade, Marchetti was one of the NFL's most feared pass rushers, and before that, he was a machine gunner during the famous Battle of the Bulge in World War II. Known as a violent hitter yet a clean player, Marchetti was a great all-around defensive end, but he was at his best in passing situations. In 1954, Marchetti protected Colts quarterbacks as a converted offensive tackle, but soon he was moved back to the other side of the line. Many teams chose to double- or even triple-team him with blockers to protect their passer, but that only opened up opportunities for Marchetti's defensive teammates. He suffered his first serious injury, a broken leg, during the Colts' dramatic 1958 NFL Championship Game victory, forcing him to miss the Pro Bowl. That was the only gap in what would have been 11 straight Pro Bowl appearances for the legendary pass rusher.

"This year, it all came true."

RAY DONALDSON ON THE 1987 SEASON

The 1976 season got off to a rocky start, as a dispute between Irsay and head coach Ted Marchibroda (Shula had left Baltimore in 1970) led to the popular coach's resignation. After Colts players voiced their disapproval and threatened to walk out, Marchibroda was reinstated. Behind Jones, the Colts went on to win the AFC East with an 11–3 record but were shut down in the playoffs by the Pittsburgh Steelers, 40–14.

Baltimore once again won the AFC East in 1977, but it took a 30–24 victory over the New England Patriots in the final game of the season to claim the divisional crown. Disappointingly, the Colts were knocked out of the playoffs in the first round, this time 37–31 in a double-overtime loss to the Oakland Raiders. Although the postseason losses were frustrating, Baltimore fans continued to believe that their team would soon break through to achieve championship glory. Unfortunately, things would get worse for the Colts before they would get better.

From 1978 to 1983, the Colts struggled, posting losing records every year. In 1983, the team was forced to trade away its top draft pick (and the first choice overall), quarterback John Elway, because he refused to play for a team that he believed showed no promise. After the 1983 season, investors from Indianapolis approached Irsay about moving his team to their city. Irsay looked at Indianapolis's Hoosier Dome, a brand-new, 60,000-seat domed stadium, and after his attempts to get a new stadium in Baltimore were rebuffed, he decided to make the move. One night, moving vans showed up at the team's Baltimore headquarters, and the Colts bolted for Indiana.

The move broke the hearts of the Baltimore faithful, but sports fans in Indiana enthusiastically welcomed the team, even as it continued to struggle in the mid-1980s. Then, in 1987, the Colts traded for star running back Eric Dickerson. Known for his graceful yet hard-nosed running style, Dickerson had established himself as one of the league's top rushers with the Los Angeles Rams.

Dickerson joined a Colts offense that already featured deep-threat wide receiver Bill Brooks and outstanding linemen Ray Donaldson and Chris Hinton. This collection of players helped carry the 1987 Colts to a 9–6 record, an AFC East title, and their first playoff appearance in 10 years. "This year, it all came true," said Donaldson. "All the dreams we had before." Unfortunately, the Colts' playoff run was short-lived, as the Browns defeated Indianapolis, 38–21.

The Blunder Bowl

When the box score shows that a football team threw three interceptions, lost four fumbles, and had its leading rusher gain only 33 yards, it's a bad sign. That's not exactly a recipe for a win—unless the team is the 1970 Baltimore Colts, and the game is Super Bowl V. Filled with sloppy play, turnovers, and even some officiating mistakes, Super Bowl V is sometimes called "The Blunder Bowl." In the second quarter, Colts quarterback Johnny Unitas threw a pass that ricocheted off Baltimore receiver Eddie Hinton's fingertips, was tipped by Dallas Cowboys defensive back Mel Renfro, and then was snatched out of the air by Baltimore tight end John Mackey for a 75-yard touchdown reception. In the third quarter, Hinton grabbed a pass that was intended for Mackey, only to fumble the ball at the 10-yard line and see it get batted through the end zone for a touchback. The Cowboys gave the ball back promptly with an interception just three plays later. Eventually, improved play by the Colts defense and a clutch kick by Jim O'Brien gave Baltimore the victory.

THE BLUNDER BOWL'S 11 COMBINED TURNOVERS REMAIN A SUPER BOWL RECORD

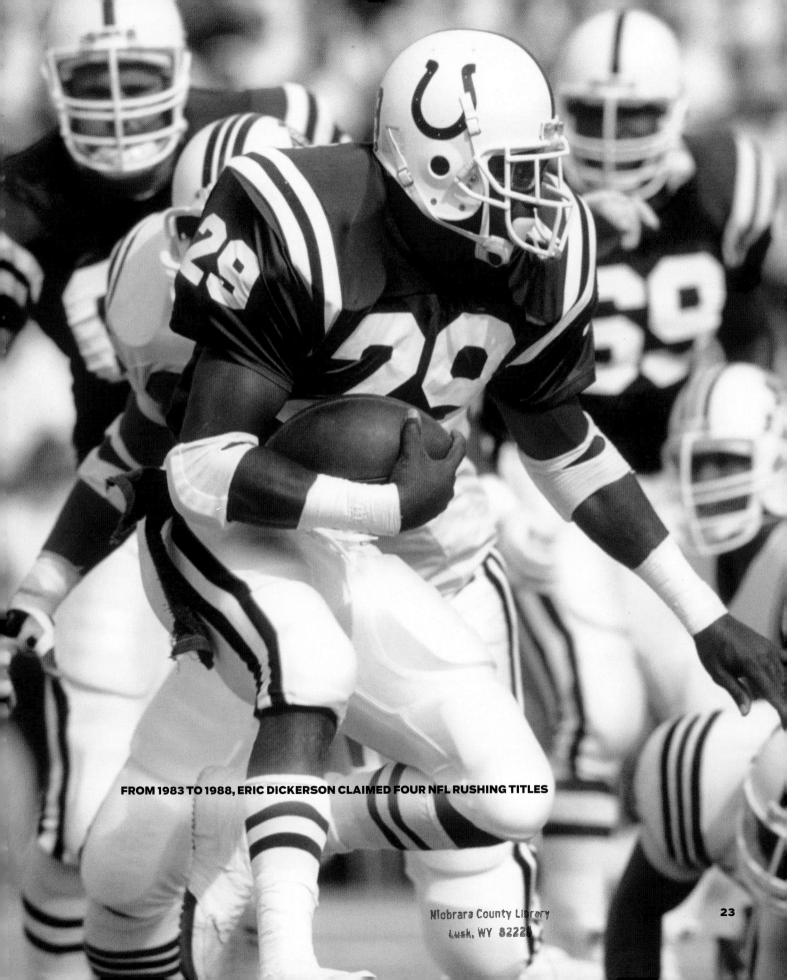

FROM 1983 TO 1988, ERIC DICKERSON CLAIMED FOUR NFL RUSHING TITLES

MARSHALL FAULK PROVED TO BE A WORTHY SUCCESSOR TO DICKERSON

In 1988, Dickerson charged for a franchise-record 1,659 yards as the Colts went 9–7 and just missed the playoffs. But after that, Indianapolis began to stumble. Over the next two seasons, the Colts went 8–8 and 7–9. In 1991, the team collapsed completely with an embarrassing 1–15 record. It was time to rebuild the Colts.

In 1992, Ted Marchibroda, who had coached the Colts in Baltimore, was hired to re-energize the franchise in Indianapolis. Marchibroda believed that coaching was "a 24-hour-a-day job. No motivating speech is going to make a difference. You have to work with your football team every minute to get it ready to play on Sunday."

Marchibroda's commitment paid off as the Colts jumped to 9–7 in 1992. The team slumped to 4–12 a year later, but Indianapolis then made two key off-season moves that would give the team a major boost. First, it signed veteran quarterback Jim Harbaugh. Then it drafted Marshall Faulk—an all-purpose running back known for his quick acceleration and shifty moves—in the first round of the 1994 NFL Draft.

In 1995, these players propelled the Colts back to the playoffs for a magical run. First, they upset the defending AFC champion Chargers 35–20. Then they beat the powerful Kansas City Chiefs 10–7. The excitement finally came to an end in the AFC Championship Game, when the Colts lost a 20–16 heartbreaker to the Steelers. On the last play of the game, Harbaugh launched a "Hail Mary" pass that was nearly caught by Colts receiver Aaron Bailey for a touchdown.

The Midnight Move

The early 1980s were a low point for the Baltimore Colts. After several seasons of few victories and low fan attendance, the once-proud franchise's best hope was to build a new stadium that would attract fans and generate increased revenue. But the Colts' owner, Robert Irsay, struggled to convince the city of Baltimore to help the team by funding that new stadium, and he threatened to move the Colts. On March 28, 1984, the state of Maryland passed an eminent domain law that would have allowed the city of Baltimore to claim ownership of the team. Afraid that his franchise and his investment were in danger, Irsay quickly agreed to move the Colts to Indianapolis. Under the cover of night, all team property was loaded into Mayflower Transit Company moving trucks. On the morning of March 30, 1984, Baltimore fans were stunned to discover that they no longer had a team. The Colts began a new era in Indianapolis, and Baltimore was left longing for an NFL franchise until 1996, when the Cleveland Browns moved there and became the Baltimore Ravens.

FIFTEEN MAYFLOWER TRUCKS ARRIVED AT BALTIMORE HEADQUARTERS AT 2:00 A.M.

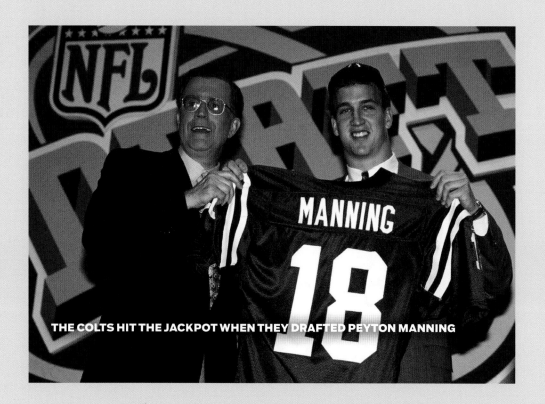

THE COLTS HIT THE JACKPOT WHEN THEY DRAFTED PEYTON MANNING

Mora and Manning

T he Colts rebounded from the demoralizing finish to the 1995 season with a 9–7 record and another trip to the playoffs in 1996. A matchup against Pittsburgh in round one gave the Colts a chance to avenge the previous year's defeat, but the powerful Steelers overwhelmed the young Colts, 42–14. When the Colts slipped to 3–13 in 1997, the team was put in the hands of former New Orleans Saints head coach Jim Mora. With Mora at the helm, the Colts used the first overall pick in the 1998 NFL Draft to add a new quarterback: University of Tennessee star Peyton Manning, the son of former NFL quarterback Archie Manning.

Neither Mora nor Manning could yank the Colts out of the AFC East cellar in 1998, as Indianapolis again posted a miserable 3–13 record. Manning showed signs of stardom, though, and began to build a great on-field relationship with speedy receiver Marvin Harrison that would last for many years. He also began cultivating a relationship with the Colts' coaching staff. "He's the kind of guy who wants to be coached," Coach Mora said

WITH MANNING UNDER CENTER, JIM MORA REBUILT THE COLTS INTO AN AFC POWER

John Mackey

TIGHT END / COLTS SEASONS: 1963–71 / HEIGHT: 6-FOOT-2 / WEIGHT: 224 POUNDS

In the early 1960s, tight ends were used mainly as extra blockers on the offensive line. John Mackey added a whole new element to the position with his spectacular ball-catching skills and field-stretching speed. In fact, Mackey was so fast that the Colts even used him as a kickoff return specialist. His athleticism and speed created headaches for opposing defenses and helped Mackey make it to the Pro Bowl five times throughout his career. During Super Bowl V, after the 1970 season, Mackey was part of one of the most memorable plays in Super Bowl history. Colts quarterback Johnny Unitas tried to complete a pass to wide receiver Eddie Hinton, only to have Hinton deflect the ball. The ball then brushed the fingers of a Dallas Cowboys defensive back and ended up in Mackey's waiting arms. Mackey took his lucky find 75 yards for a touchdown, putting the Colts in position to eventually win the game on a last-second field goal. Such plays helped Mackey elevate the profile of the tight end position and earned him induction into the Pro Football Hall of Fame in 1992.

EDGERRIN JAMES WAS THE NFL'S LEADING RUSHER HIS FIRST TWO SEASONS

of Manning. "You can't overwork him. He's like a sponge. He wants to do the best he can, and he wants you to give him all that you have to give him."

With budding superstars at quarterback and wide receiver, the Colts continued to add talent. In 1999, they traded Faulk to the St. Louis Rams and then selected explosive University of Miami running back Edgerrin James in the NFL Draft. Indianapolis also bulked up its defense by signing veteran linebacker Cornelius Bennett and end Chad Bratzke.

The off-season moves paid immediate dividends, and the Colts skyrocketed to a remarkable 13–3 record in 1999, claiming the division crown for the first time since 1987. Manning, Harrison, and James became one of the most feared offensive trios in the NFL: Manning threw for more than 4,000 yards, Harrison topped all NFL receivers with 1,663 yards, and James led the league in rushing with 1,553 yards. Despite all of that success, the season came to a disappointing end in the playoffs, as the Colts lost 19–16 to the Tennessee Titans.

When the Colts slumped to 6–10 in 2001, Coach Mora was replaced by Tony Dungy, a defense-minded coach who had previously built the Tampa Bay Buccaneers into a powerhouse. The Colts surged to 10–6 in their first season under Dungy, thanks in part to young defensive end Dwight Freeney, receiver

Reggie Wayne, and tight end Marcus Pollard. Unfortunately, the season again ended on a bitter note when Indianapolis was drubbed 41–0 by the New York Jets in the playoffs.

In 2003, the Colts bolstered their already fearsome passing game by drafting tight end Dallas Clark out of the University of Iowa. They also got a big boost from kicker Mike Vanderjagt, who set a league record by going an entire season and postseason without missing a field goal or an extra-point attempt. Thanks in part to Clark and Vanderjagt, the Colts assembled a 12–4 record. Unfortunately, Indianapolis came up short once again in its bid to reach the Super Bowl, losing to the New England Patriots in the AFC Championship Game—a loss that began an intense rivalry between the clubs that would last for years.

REGGIE WAYNE WAS PART OF AN IMPRESSIVE FLEET OF INDIANAPOLIS RECEIVERS

Lucky Leg

After faltering in the playoffs for four straight seasons, the Colts entered the 2006 season hoping to finally get back to the Super Bowl—and hoping that their new kicker, Adam Vinatieri, would help them get there. Vinatieri had played in the Super Bowl four times with the New England Patriots and twice had kicked the game-winning points through the uprights in the waning seconds of the game. His accuracy was so renowned that he had earned the nickname "Automatic Adam"; his ability to remain calm in stressful situations had given some teammates cause to call him "Iceman" as well. Even after Vinatieri's lucky leg helped lead the Colts back to the Super Bowl, where he kicked three field goals as the Colts beat the Bears 29–17, he held his emotions in check. "My favorite ring is my next ring," he said after joining an elite group of players with four Super Bowl wins. When the Colts marched to the Super Bowl in 2009, Vinatieri had an opportunity to become just the second player to win a fifth ring— but Indianapolis lost to New Orleans, 31–17.

ADAM VINATIERI PLAYED HIS 17TH NFL SEASON IN 2012 AT THE AGE OF 40

BOB SANDERS WAS JUST 5-FOOT-8 BUT HIT LIKE A MUCH BIGGER PLAYER

In 2004, Manning enjoyed one of the greatest seasons any quarterback has ever had. He was given the NFL's Most Valuable Player (MVP) award after throwing a league-record 49 touchdown passes and racking up 4,557 passing yards. "It's difficult to pick one player out of the league and determine who is the most valuable," said Coach Dungy. "But Peyton sets the tempo for us. We ask a lot of him, and he's certainly delivered."

Behind Manning's record-setting performance, the Colts again won 12 games in 2004. Along the way, the wide receiver trio of Harrison, Wayne, and Brandon Stokley became the first NFL threesome to each post more than 1,000 yards and make 10 or more touchdown catches for a team in a single season. On the other side of the ball, Freeney used his frightening speed and spin moves to become the first Colts player to win the league's sack title, with 16. "Freeney gets better and better every year, and it seems like he's getting faster and faster," Titans quarterback Steve McNair said. "Sometimes you think there's something wrong with the [film] projector when you see how quick he is."

Despite all of these remarkable individual accomplishments, the Colts were still not quite ready for the Super Bowl. After beating the Denver Broncos 49–24 in their first playoff game, they were stifled by the Patriots a week later, losing 20–3. The Colts improved to a 14–2 record the next season, partly because of an improved defense that featured aggressive linebacker Cato June and hard-hitting free safety Bob Sanders. Yet despite having home-field advantage in AFC playoffs, the "Horseshoes" again came up short in the postseason, suffering a wrenching 21–18 loss to the Steelers.

MANNING PLAYED ALONGSIDE SEVERAL TALENTED RUSHERS, INCLUDING JOSEPH ADDAI

DWIGHT FREENEY COMBINED RARE SPEED WITH BRILLIANT SPIN MOVES

Super Bowl Bound

Before the start of the 2006 season, Indianapolis parted ways with Edgerrin James, opting to let the one-two punch of Dominic Rhodes and rookie Joseph Addai carry the Colts' rushing load. Indianapolis also let Vanderjagt leave as a free agent and signed clutch kicker Adam Vinatieri away from the rival Patriots. The changes achieved the desired results, as the Colts cruised to a division-topping 12–4 record and another playoff berth. In the postseason, the Colts toppled the Kansas City Chiefs by a score of 23–8, then took down the Baltimore Ravens 15–6, thanks to Vinatieri's five field goals. Once again, however, the Colts would have to defeat the Patriots if they were to reach the Super Bowl.

Behind a strong running attack from Addai and Rhodes and an 80-yard scoring drive in the fourth quarter engineered by Manning, the Colts finally topped the Patriots, winning the AFC Championship Game 38–34 and securing a place in Super Bowl XLI. The showdown, played in Miami, was to be a historic one, as it was the first Super

SUPER BOWL XLI BETWEEN THE COLTS AND THE BEARS WAS A RAIN-SOAKED BATTLE

Marvin Harrison

WIDE RECEIVER / COLTS SEASONS: 1996–2008 / HEIGHT: 6 FEET / WEIGHT: 175 POUNDS

In the NFL today, it's common to see wide receivers competing over who can come up with the most outlandish touchdown celebrations and crowd-pleasing dances. Yet while many receivers spent time practicing their dance moves, Marvin Harrison quietly kept breaking records. There was very little that was flashy about Harrison. He played smart, ran precise routes, and caught passes—a lot of them. Over the course of his career, he and quarterback Peyton Manning teamed up to become one of the most successful "pitch-and-catch" tandems in NFL history. The pair knew each other so well that, with just a look, they could switch plays to exploit a flaw in the defense. Although Harrison became the Colts' record holder in nearly every receiving category, the quiet star preferred to let his play speak for him, letting more outgoing teammates get most of the media attention. Donovan McNabb, a teammate of Harrison's at Syracuse University and longtime quarterback for the Philadelphia Eagles, appreciated his style, saying, "So many receivers go throughout their career talking about how great they are, and how much they're going to do. Marvin just does it."

Bowl to feature two teams led by African American head coaches. Tony Dungy brought his Colts to face Lovie Smith and his Chicago Bears.

Bears receiver Devin Hester returned the game's opening kickoff 92 yards across a rain-sodden field for a quick touchdown and an early lead for Chicago. After a sloppy first half that featured six total turnovers, the Colts held a 16–14 lead. In the second half, thanks to Manning's consistent play, a dominant running game, and an opportunistic defense that seemed to stay one step ahead of Chicago, the Colts shook off the rain and the Bears to win 29–17 and finally bring the Lombardi Trophy to Indianapolis. Coach Dungy praised his team after the victory, saying, "This may not have been our best team in

THE COLTS' CHAMPIONSHIP WAS THE BIGGEST SPORTS TITLE IN INDIANAPOLIS HISTORY

LUCAS OIL STADIUM HAS BEEN CALLED "THE HOUSE THAT MANNING BUILT"

five years, but it was the closest and the most connected—and it showed in the way we played."

The Colts kept their momentum going the next two seasons. In 2007, they went 13–3 to earn a first-round bye in the playoffs. There would be no Super Bowl repeat, though. Injuries to such stars as Freeney and Harrison crippled the team in the postseason, and Indianapolis fell to the Chargers, 28–24. After a slow start in 2008 that included losing their first two home games in Indianapolis's brand-new Lucas Oil Stadium, the Colts came on strong late in the season to finish 12–4 and earn a Wild Card spot in the playoffs. Unfortunately for Indianapolis fans, the Colts were again stymied by the Chargers in the postseason, losing 23–17.

That game turned out to be the last for Coach Dungy, who retired and turned the team over to assistant coach Jim Caldwell. Caldwell's Colts won their first game of the 2009 season and proceeded to court an undefeated season by winning the next 13 games as well. After Manning completed his 50,000th passing yard—becoming only the 4th player in NFL history to do so—and the team clinched the division title, Caldwell gave some of his top stars a break before the playoffs.

The well-rested Colts cruised to an easy 20–3 win over the Baltimore Ravens in the divisional round and then crushed the Jets 30–17 to win the AFC Championship Game and earn a spot in the Super Bowl again. This time, the Colts faced the surging New Orleans Saints, who were making their first-ever trip to

Orchestrated Confusion

In the early seasons of the 21st century, when the Colts broke the huddle (if they even huddled at all), they would frequently still have about 20 seconds left on the play clock. Then, as the players got into their stances, star quarterback Peyton Manning would run back and forth at the line of scrimmage, yelling and gesticulating wildly to his teammates in what looked like mass confusion. In reality, the Colts' offense, developed by coordinator Tom Moore, was not as complicated as it seemed. Manning would call two to four play options in the huddle, and then, once he'd seen the defensive alignment at the line of scrimmage, he would choose and communicate which of those plays he wanted to run. The Colts' offense became so adept at this that players could even communicate the plays with simple hand gestures. Meanwhile, Manning would go through a wide variety of calls and gestures in an attempt to confuse the defense. "My base philosophy has been that players make plays," said Moore. "As a coach, you give them a system that allows them to do that."

PEYTON MANNING WAS A MASTER OF BOTH DIRECTION AND MISDIRECTION

SAFETY ANTOINE BETHEA WAS A TWO-TIME PRO-BOWLER

a Super Bowl after flirting with an undefeated season as well. Although the Colts took the early lead and were up 17–13 midway through the third quarter, the Saints scored 18 unanswered points and won the game, 31–17.

The Colts were good again in 2010, compiling a 10–6 record that topped the AFC South Division (Indianapolis had joined the AFC South in 2002) and sent them back to the playoffs for the ninth straight season. But this time, Indianapolis was stopped by the Jets in a back-and-forth game that ended with the Jets on top by just one point, 17–16.

During the off-season, Manning underwent a pair of surgeries to repair a bulging disc in his neck and was still recovering when the 2011 season started. As Manning watched, the Colts lost one game after another in devastating fashion. Although there were rumors that the star quarterback might be cleared to return before the end of the season, Indianapolis had no chance of returning to the playoffs after losing its first 12 games. Manning, who stood on the sidelines offering any assistance possible to the string of quarterbacks called upon to replace him, felt helpless as he watched the Colts' downward spiral. "Being 0–12 is frustrating for everybody in our building," he said. "It's disappointing. I hate everything about it." Indianapolis salvaged the season with two wins—enough to avoid the humiliation of going winless but not enough to lift the players' spirits. That poor finish put the team in prime position for the 2012 NFL Draft, though, and the Colts chose college standout Andrew Luck from Stanford with the top overall pick to replace Manning at quarterback. Meanwhile, Manning was picked up by the Denver Broncos, and a new era dawned in Indianapolis.

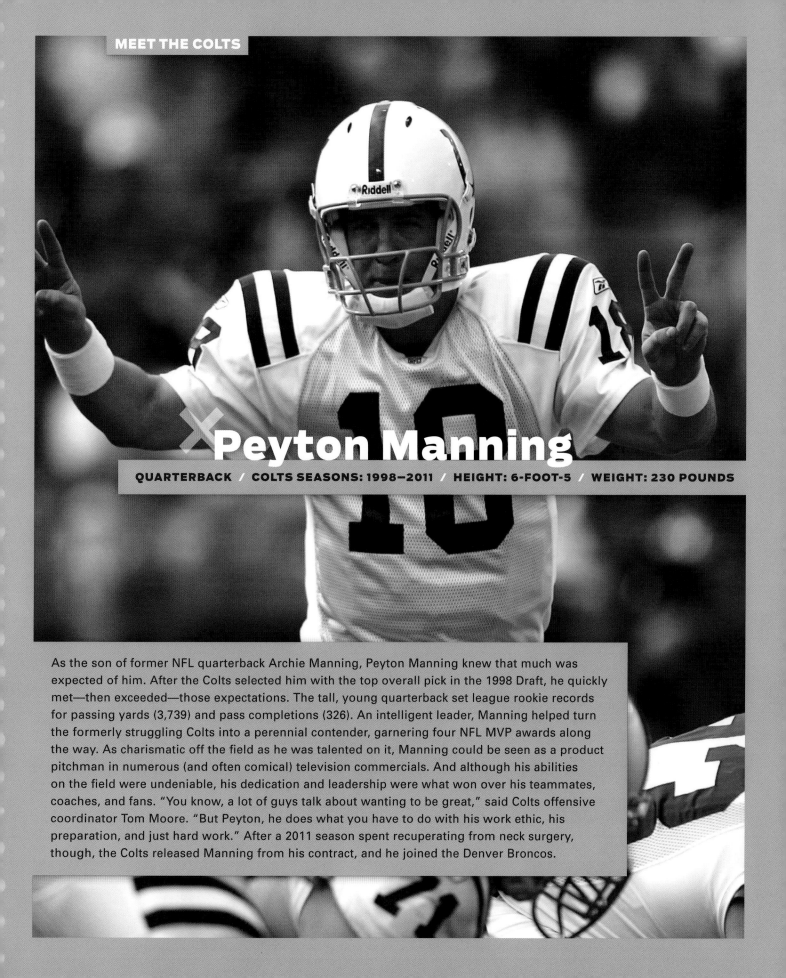

Peyton Manning

QUARTERBACK / COLTS SEASONS: 1998—2011 / HEIGHT: 6-FOOT-5 / WEIGHT: 230 POUNDS

As the son of former NFL quarterback Archie Manning, Peyton Manning knew that much was expected of him. After the Colts selected him with the top overall pick in the 1998 Draft, he quickly met—then exceeded—those expectations. The tall, young quarterback set league rookie records for passing yards (3,739) and pass completions (326). An intelligent leader, Manning helped turn the formerly struggling Colts into a perennial contender, garnering four NFL MVP awards along the way. As charismatic off the field as he was talented on it, Manning could be seen as a product pitchman in numerous (and often comical) television commercials. And although his abilities on the field were undeniable, his dedication and leadership were what won over his teammates, coaches, and fans. "You know, a lot of guys talk about wanting to be great," said Colts offensive coordinator Tom Moore. "But Peyton, he does what you have to do with his work ethic, his preparation, and just hard work." After a 2011 season spent recuperating from neck surgery, though, the Colts released Manning from his contract, and he joined the Denver Broncos.

ANDREW LUCK EXCEEDED EXPECTATIONS BY LEADING THE COLTS TO AN 11—5 MARK IN 2012

DONALD BROWN SHOWED STEADY IMPROVEMENT AS A COLTS BALLCARRIER

Luck's rookie season rivaled that of his predecessor's. He threw for even more yards (4,374 versus Manning's 3,739 in 1998) for 23 touchdowns on the season and led his team to second place in the AFC South. All this was done under the watchful eye of interim head coach Bruce Arians, who stepped in when new hire Chuck Pagano had to undergo treatment for leukemia and miss most of 2012. Pagano made a triumphant return in time for the final game, announcing that his cancer was in remission. The Colts celebrated the good news with a win against the Houston Texans and prepared to face the Ravens in a playoff game for the AFC Wild Card slot. Baltimore bridled the Colts in that contest, though, and the only Indianapolis points scored came off the foot of the capable Vinatieri. Still, looking ahead to 2013, an optimistic Coach Pagano said, "The players have set high expectations for themselves . . . the bar is really high. And we're just going to keep working the process, continuing to build the monster . . . and move forward."

If history has taught the Colts anything, it's that losing streaks don't last forever. The Colts' six-decade tradition in the NFL includes five thrilling championship seasons as well as a few disappointing downtimes. But through it all, the fans have supported their hometown heroes. And they are anxious to expand their bulging trophy case to make room for another championship trophy when the time comes.